SEAMM-JASANI

8 ESSENTIAL MOVEMENTS

SEAMM-JASANI

8 ESSENTIAL MOVEMENTS

RELAXATION, STRETCHING, AND BREATHING
FROM THE ART OF ETERNAL YOUTH

Asanaro
In the year of the Asubuio

ISBN: 978-1-257-32202-2

Translation by: Asanaro, Amlom, and Yemado
Drawings: Asanaro
Edited by: Stephanie Bruce
Photography: Yemado (www.yemado.com)
Front Cover: Seamm-Jasani Seminar in Norway
Rear Cover: Asanaro in Europe
Cover Design: Yemado

Seamm-Jasani: 8 Essential Movements
Aya Publishing
Printed in USA
First English Edition
2011

www.asanaro.com
asanaro@boabom.org

TABLE OF CONTENTS

Dedicated to the new seeds:
Students of Boabom & Seamm-Jasani
from the Roof of the World
to the End of the Earth

Introduction

This book is a summary of basic movements, or *Jass-U*, that are used, in practice, to complement *Seamm-Jasani*, the Art of Eternal Youth. *Seamm-Jasani* is developed through gentle exercises, breathing techniques (pranayama), and coordinations designed to stimulate relaxation and energy, as well as physical and mental health. *Seamm-Jasani* is part of a system of teaching called Boabom (རྦོ་ལ་རྦོ། or Boabom Tsa-lung: རྦོ་ལ་རྩ་རླུང་། in Tibetan).

A more specific term for the type of movements described in this book is Jass-U, or "the Art of Awakening," as it helps the student to recover and balance their energy. With practice, the student feels prepared to go about their daily life with strength, vitality, and a positive mood. It is an excellent method to improve one's health and recover from stressful situations, making it very attractive for people who explore alternative medicine. Moreover, this technique is adaptable to individuals of any age or physical condition, making it ideal for the infirm, the elderly, and those suffering or recovering from serious illness.

Many students of Yoga (Hatha Yoga in particular) have found the art of *Seamm-Jasani* to be an excellent complement, even an alternative, to more traditional Yoga, because they can replace complicated positions and asanas, some that are impossible for many people, with gentle, energizing movements and steps.

The roots of *Boabom, Seamm-Jasani* and the *Jass-U* are in ancient Tibet, where they were taught hermetically from generation to generation, as a family tradition, directly from teacher to student. Circumstances brought this system to the West in the 1960s and now, from the outset of our new century, a group of experienced teachers based in Boston (USA) has been working to formalize this teaching as a universal, open school, beyond culture or religion.

Used by doctors and health professionals as an effective method for recovering from physical injuries and improving psychological well-being, the Boabom Arts have been taught with success in the USA, South America, Europe, and Asia.

The idea of this manual comes in response to the need of a large number of people who wish to know this Art and begin studying it in as easy a way as is possible. Thus, this text is a basic guide for daily practice. It contains eight essential movements, easy to learn and easy to practice for fifteen minutes every morning. As a complement, this book includes the first basic coordinative form from *Seamm-Jasani*.

All of these techniques are detailed in the book *The Secret Art of Seamm-Jasani: 58 Movements for Eternal Youth*, which has been translated into 7 languages and has become widely popular, with student-readers from around the globe. It contains a more thorough and complete system (including 35 movements of *Jass-U* and 23 of *Seamm-Jasani*), so any student who develops a deeper interest can continue their progress in that book. For interested and curious students, there is also the book *The Secret Art of Boabom*, which develops these Arts from the point of view of defense, developing a *Jass-U* of strength and endurance in addition to movements of self-defense.

But all of that lays ahead; what is important now is to start with the essential, so…

Welcome to Seamm-Jasani: 8 Essential Movements!

Asanaro

Before You Begin

Find a quiet place for your practice. It does not have to be large, just a comfortable room with good ventilation. Wear loose, comfortable clothes, and try to do your exercises before breakfast, or on an empty stomach, as it is not good exercise just after eating.

If you ever feel nervous or worried and you would like to relieve your stress using just one movement in particular, the fourth movement (the Breathing Technique of the Great Circle) is the best; repeat it just a few times under any circumstance and you will feel much better.

General Basic Movement: Relaxing and Loosening Up

Gently relax your arms and legs. We will do this between movements to release tension and keep ourselves from getting tired; when this book says *relax,* this is what we mean. Walk in place, gently and comfortably moving your arms and legs in order to release the basic tensions from your extremities. Clear your mind and imagine yourself walking through beautiful fields.

Movement 1
Turning Arms - Forward

This is the first movement of the first cycle, and it is based on a very simple mechanism. Continue to relax your legs (pretending to walk just as before), while extending your arms in front of you with your fingers pointing out, turning them as if turning a light bulb in and out of a socket on the wall in front of you, in a circular movement to the front, in and out.

All of these movements will channel the energy from your extremities, each in a different way. Now the muscles are working in a circular pattern, twisting. Your legs should always remain moving.

The drawing shows a lateral view of the movement, as does the detail of the hand.

Count slowly to 12, then begin the next movement.

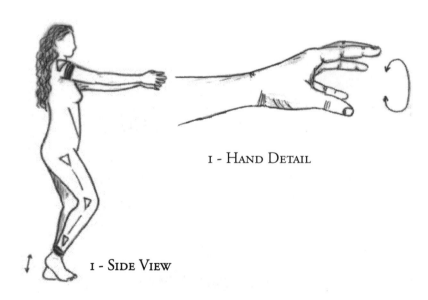

1 - HAND DETAIL

1 - SIDE VIEW

Movement 2
Turning Arms – Lateral

Continue to relax as described above, while extending your arms to both sides and making the same movements with your hands as in the previous exercise, that of twisting a light bulb, except that now the sockets are to your sides.

To begin to give life to your lower zone, lower your body a little bit, bending at the knees as if you were about to sit down, then bringing yourself back up. If you want to challenge yourself a little, try to lower yourself some more before going back up very slowly. At the beginning it is enough if you only descend a little, bending your knees just a bit. Though this may seem easy at first, your legs will begin to work in a different way than they are used to.

Count to 12 and then begin the next movement.

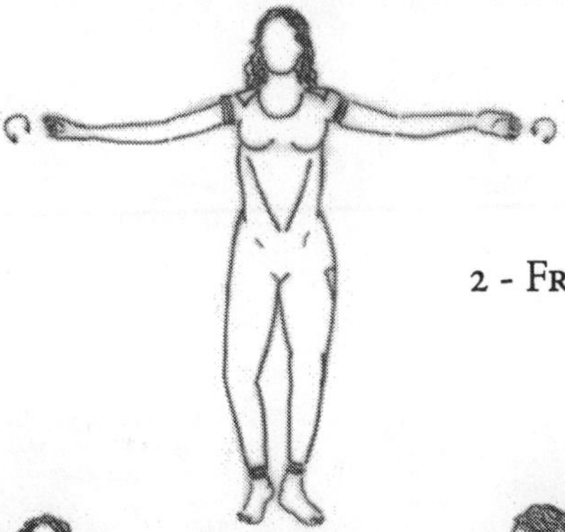

2 - Front

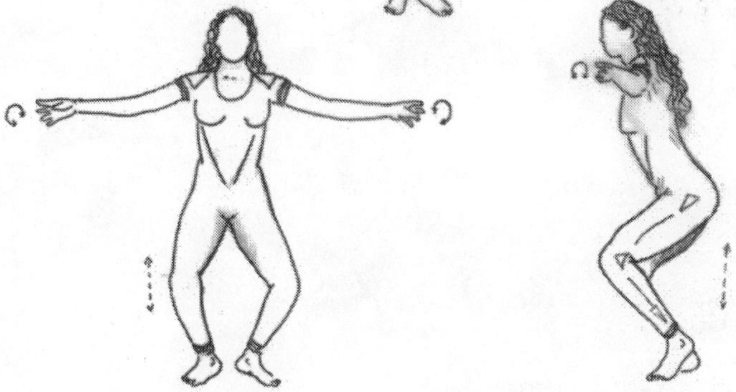

2 - Front and Side, Descending

Movement 3
Turning Arms – High

Continue relaxing. Now raise your arms above your head while continuing the same movement with your hands, as if twisting a light bulb, this time with your hands pointing at the ceiling. Now lower yourself, just as in the previous exercise.

The drawings on the left describe the movement of the hands, while the drawings on the right add the movement of lowering yourself with your legs.

If properly executed this you will feel as if you are making a great effort with your arms; do not worry, this is completely normal.

Count to 12 and continue.

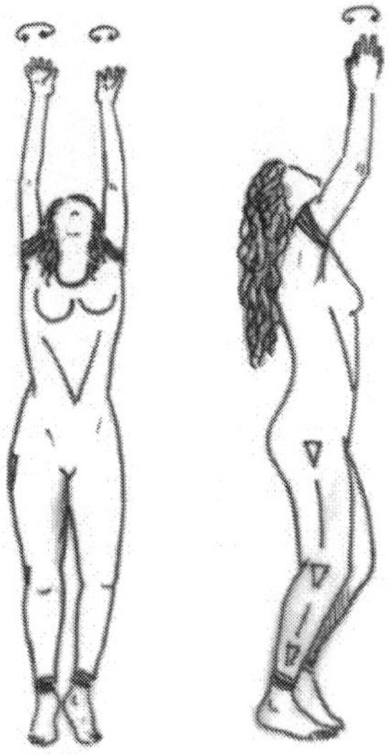

3
FRONT & SIDE VIEWS

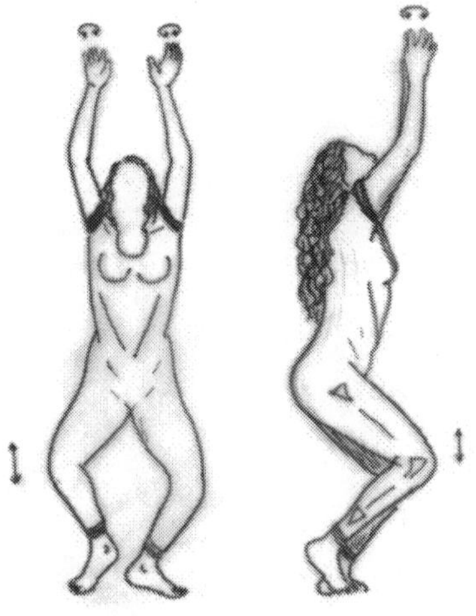

3
FRONT & SIDE VIEWS
DESCENDING

Movement 4
Breathing Technique of the Great Circle

This movement requires particular attention as you learn it, for the understanding of this breathing technique is related to, and vital for, all the rest of the movements.

The breathing technique (pranayama) will be explained in three stages: The first will show the physical movements involved, called the External Movement; the second analyzes the position of the breathing tracts as well as the sound required for proper execution of the technique, which together we call the Internal Movement. Finally, we will unify the internal and external stages.

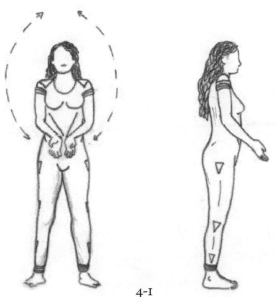

4-1
FRONT & SIDE VIEWS

Stage One:

Stand normally, your back and shoulders straight but unexaggerated, with your feet at shoulder width. Place your hands as shown in drawing 4-1, slightly in front of your body.

Now move them upwards, in a smooth and harmonious circle, as shown in drawing 4-2, until your hands are horizontal and raised above your head, as in 4-3. As you raise your hands lean your upper body slightly backward in order to produce the maximum natural extension of the chest wall. Then return your hands, with the same motion, to where they began, and you have traced the same circle in reverse.

Make sure to pay special attention to the drawings, as they show three stages of the circle: beginning, middle, and its fullest extension, from both the front and lateral views. To return, simply reverse the movement (4-3 → 4-2 → 4-1).

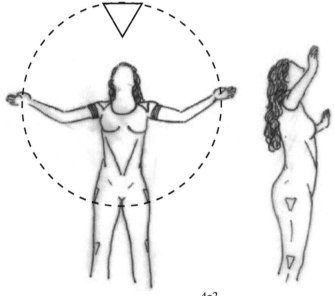

4-2
FRONT & SIDE VIEWS

Stage Two:

In this part we examine in detail the position and flow of our respiratory system.

THE INHALATION: Begin by putting your tongue against your palate and inhaling through your nose. You will feel a slight pressure in your nasal cavities as a natural result. When inhaling, we produce a specific sound (nnnsss...) by applying a slight force as the air enters. The sound must be audible and loud enough to be heard in a quiet place from at least five or six feet away. This is important, for it is by the audible sound that we know when the execution of the breathing technique is correct. This is as the old teachings say, "Know the sound of your body, know the sound of life."

You must also try to extend the sound for as long as possible, using the pressure you are exerting to force the air to enter as slowly as possible in order to filter and heat it enough for its coming *digestion*. All the while you should expand both chest and stomach as much as you can; this serves to lower and stretch the diaphragm.

THE CONTAINMENT: Now, you must hold the air, with all of its nutrients, for about five seconds, while holding your hands still, above your head.

THE EXHALATION: This is the third and final phase of the breathing technique. It uses what we call a high exhalation, which is as follows: Lower your tongue down from your palate and exhale through your mouth, rounding your lips and forcing the air along the throat with a gentle pressure, making an "hhhaaa..." sound. The natural pressure of this phase is exerted in the throat, and with this we clean out any dirt and small particles of dust that settle in our breathing tract. The rounding of the lips also helps to create the sound of this exhalation, in between the long 'a' and 'o' sounds, and this too must be audible from at least five or six feet away. If it is inaudible, it will not result in the benefits that we seek.

Concentrate on the details, breathe well, and with practice you will see positive results.

When inhaling and exhaling, you must extend the movement as much as possible each and every time. Even though it is normal that in the first sessions your lung capacity will be small, you will discover with time that the lungs are muscles that can be developed, stretched, and enlarged just as any other, except that in the case of the lungs the benefits are noticeable throughout your entire body.

This exercise will have the same effect on you as if you replaced a car's dirty carburetor with a brand new one… Now that it is clean its capacity is greatly increased, and with such modifications over time your old VW Bug will be transformed into quite a sports car.

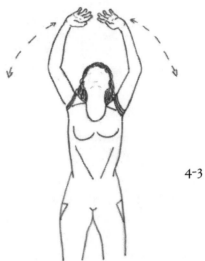

4-3

Stage Three:

Now that you understand the internal and external aspects of this breathing, we will join them and practice the entire technique, so that we may use it with all of the movements.   Follow this sequence:

1—Standing normally, with your hands as they are in drawing 4-1, put your tongue against your palate and inhale, making the nasal "nnnsss…" sound while slowly raising your arms, tracing a circle with your hands (4-2) until, as they are directly above your head (4-3), you finish your inhalation.

2—Once your hands are above your head and you have finished inhaling, contain the air in your lungs for about five seconds, while keeping your hands up. Your thorax and diaphragm are now completely extended (4-3).

3—Lower your tongue from your palate, round your lips, and exhale with gentle pressure along the back of your throat while lowering your arms along the same circle as before. Breathe out slowly, making the "hhhaaa..." sound from your throat, your arms moving as slowly as your breath, returning to their initial position just as the sound stops. When you are finished, rest.

This technique must be repeated two or three times. It serves as an excellent form of relaxation, and a good way to release tension and stress in negative situations. Always keep this breathing technique in mind, as it will help you clear your mind, calm down, and escape a nervous mental state.

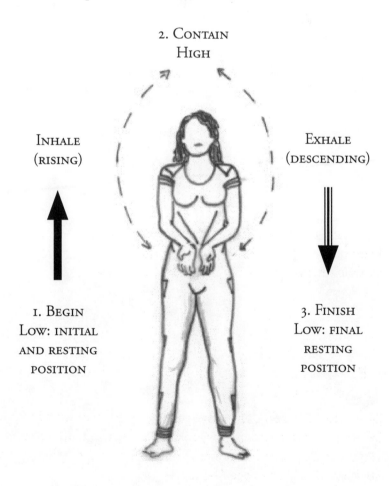

2. CONTAIN
HIGH

INHALE
(RISING)

EXHALE
(DESCENDING)

1. BEGIN
LOW: INITIAL
AND RESTING
POSITION

3. FINISH
LOW: FINAL
RESTING
POSITION

Movement 5
Swimming Ahead

Relax in the normal manner, then bring your hands to your sides, as shown in the first drawing. Lean a little to the front and move your hands forward, right over left, with your palms up. Lean forward, bending at the hips and keeping your back straight, as you continue to extend your arms. As your arms reach their fullest extension, turn your palms to face outward and move your hands horizontally, as if swimming, and trace two circles, finally moving your body back to a normal standing position as your hands come back to their starting position. Relax, then repeat the complete sequence.

Pretend we are swimming in an imaginary ocean: the waves refresh us, gently touching us as we glide through the warm water. This makes us feel happy, relieved, and renewed, as we exercise our imagination!

Repeat this movement 12 times, then continue to the next.

5 - 1   5 - 2 INHALE

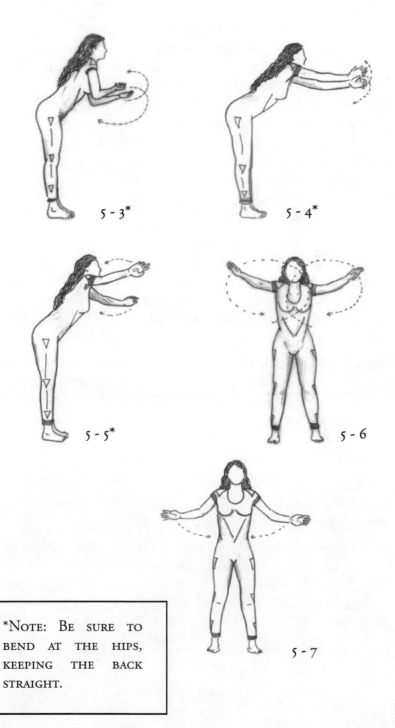

5 - 3*

5 - 4*

5 - 5*

5 - 6

5 - 7

*NOTE: BE SURE TO BEND AT THE HIPS, KEEPING THE BACK STRAIGHT.

Movement 6
The Machine

Begin standing normally, with your hands in front of you (6-1). Now bring your hands to your sides in two short movements, accompanied with a double inhalation (nnnsss... nnnsss...) (6-2). Now, bend forward at the hips, your torso led down by your straightening arms (6-3), the palms of your hands facing up. Stretch downward, combining two short extensions with a double exhalation (hhhaaa... hhhaaa...). Do not bend your knees, and try to touch the floor with the two short extensions, though you should never force anything.

Now bring yourself back to the initial position, with your hands at your sides, inhaling twice. Immediately repeat the downward movement, including the two downward hand movements and the double exhalation, and again straighten your body while inhaling twice, continuing this process without losing continuity.

Use your imagination with this movement, and we will pretend to be a machine, or the engine of a train, slowly speeding up while our body remains firm and in control. As you feel more confident with this exercise you can move faster, going up and down, inhaling twice and exhaling twice with two short extensions of our arms. Now you are strong, your engine has broken through its inertia and every time we move faster and faster!

After 12 or 20 seconds we calmly slow down, relax, and finally stop.

With this movement we have broken up our solid energy and forced it to rush throughout our whole body. Always remember not to over-exert yourself, and at the same time make sure to keep it interesting for you, as everyone needs to work according to her or his own body.

Now relax your arms and legs normally, and continue with the next movement.

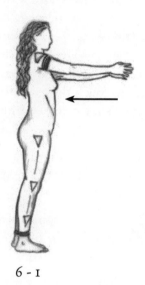

6 - 1

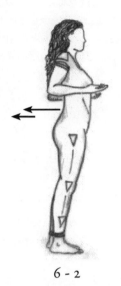

6 - 2

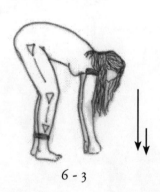

6 - 3

6 - 4

Movement 7
To the Earth

Begin this movement in the same position as the last, standing up straight, with your arms in front of you. Bring your hands to your sides with a long inhalation (nnnsss...). Now, bending at your hips, slowly exhale (hhhaaa...) as you lower your torso, until your head is down and your arms are hanging. Inhale again, stretching farther and farther as you try to touch the ground with the backs of your hands. You should feel a gentle warmth, a tickling in the backs of your arms and head.

Exhale again as you slowly return to the initial position. You have just brought a lot of blood into your head and upper extremities, so a little dizziness is completely normal.

This technique is quite special and, if you like you can do it every morning to help you awaken and renew your brain. You will blush quickly, having just received an excellent, stimulating vitamin!

Repeat the entire movement three times, then go on to the next movement.

7

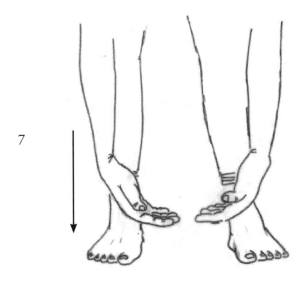

Movement 8
To the Sky

Stand normally, your arms relaxed at your sides (8-1). Slowly raise your arms above your head as you inhale (8-2). When your arms are fully extended, exhale, but keep them raised above your head. Now inhale again, trying to touch the sky or ceiling (8-3, 8-4), straightening your body as much as you can, trying to reach beyond! Finally, lower your arms as you exhale slowly.

As with the previous movement, it is normal to feel a slight heat or tickling in your upper extremities: don't worry, it is just your body waking up.

Stretch three times, and continue.

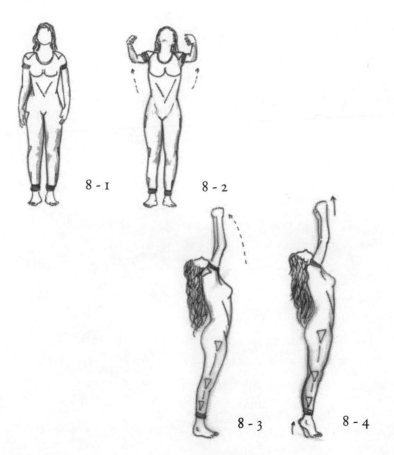

8 - 1   8 - 2   8 - 3   8 - 4

Appendix:
Seamm-Jasani Form: *Dawn*

As a complement to our eight movements, you can add this form from *Seamm-Jasani*, a coordination that fluidly joins breathing and movement with meditation and awakening.

This form is called *Dawn*, for its movements extend like the arms of the morning sun. Follow these steps to awaken your body-mind. This form is also taught in my book *The Secret Art of Seamm-Jasani*, where it can be studied in more detail.

1. Initial Position: Begin with your hands resting, left over right (A-1).

2. Bring your arms at your sides (A-2), shoulders straight. The hands are open, as if holding a small ball between your fingers. Open your left foot diagonally.

3. Slowly bring both arms forward (A-3), turning the hands inward with the little finger pointing up, still in the same hand position. Inhale (nnnsss...) as you project your arms. When you have finished stretching, contain your breath for few seconds.

4. Lift your right foot (A-4), then move it to the right, in a straight line and landing with the foot, very softly, exhaling at the same time and keeping both arms extended to the front (the arms remain still while tje leg moves).

5. In this position (A-5) the legs form a gentle arc, with the feet angled slightly open and the back straight.

6. Inhale as you return your arms to your sides (A-6).

7. Exhale, stretch your arms out to your sides (A-7), as if pushing two walls away from you.

8. Now we repeat the same movements but in reverse. Inhale as you bring your hands back to your sides (A-8).

9. Again stretch both your arms to the front as you exhale (A-9). When they are fully extended, hold them in that position.

10. Now, turn your right foot inward, inhale gently, and return

(A-10), lifting your leg, lowering your foot, and finally placing it next to the left leg. The arms should remain stretched forward.

11. Now exhale, returning both your arms toward your body (A-11).

12. Finally, turn your left foot to face forward as you lower your hands into the initial position (A-12). We have returned to the beginning, and can now start anew, refreshed by the warmth of the morning sun!

And now we have finished the Seamm-Jasani Form: *Dawn.*

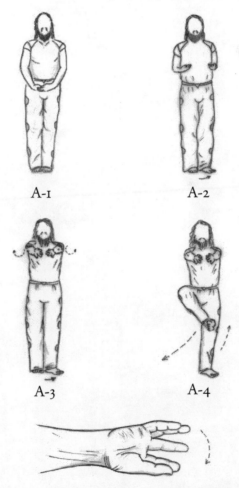

A-1   A-2

A-3   A-4

DETAIL OF THE POSITION OF THE HANDS WHEN EXTENDED.

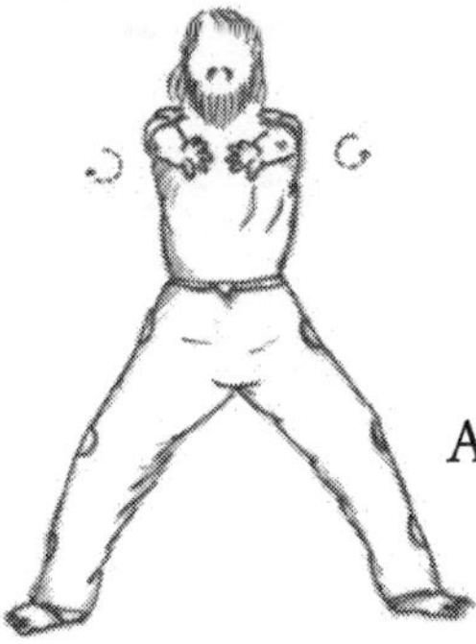

A-5

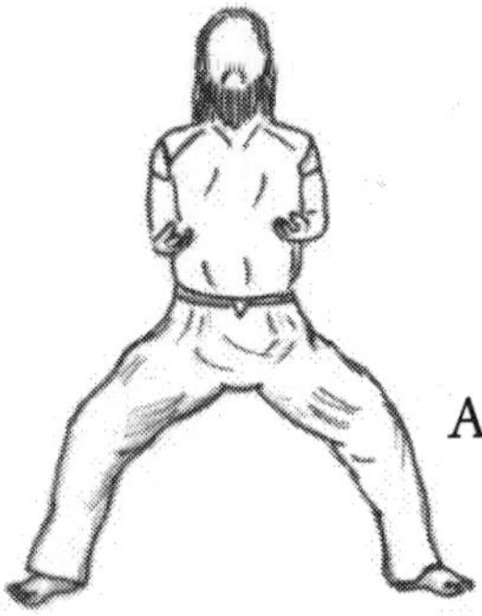

A-6

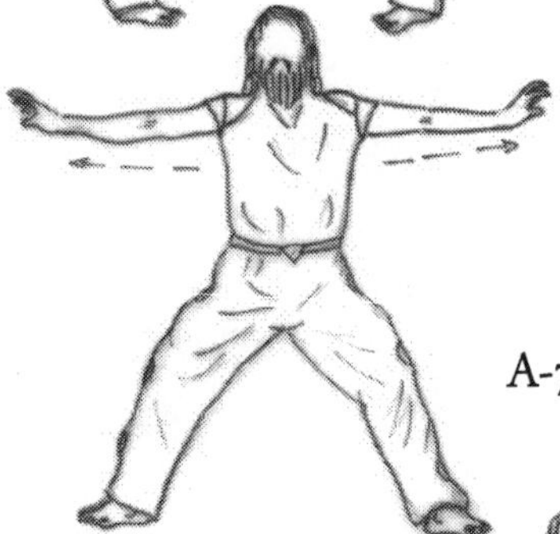

A-7

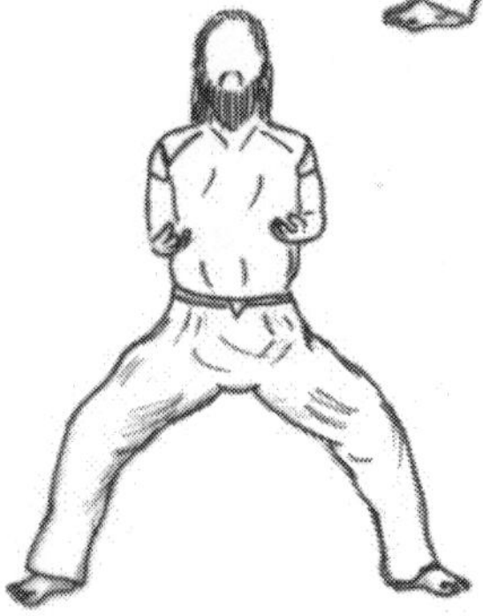

A-8

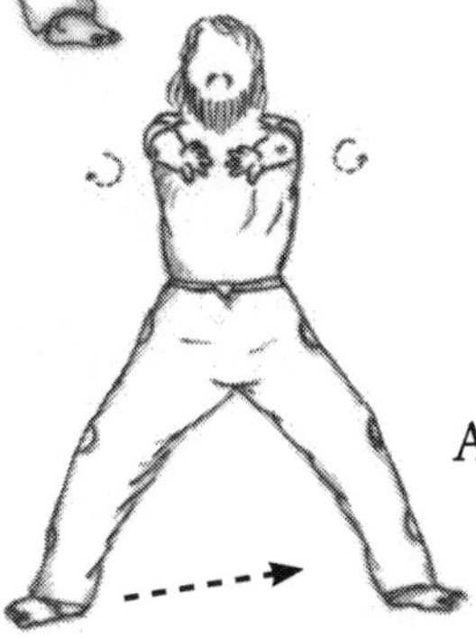

A-9

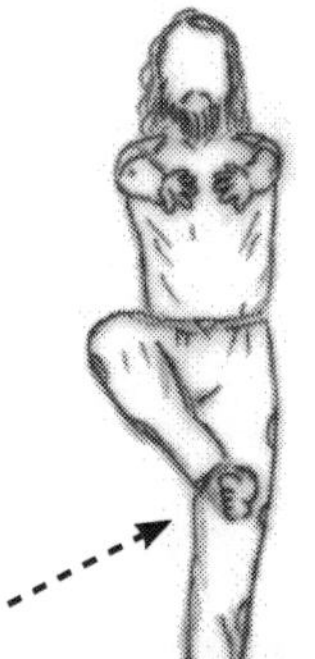

A-10

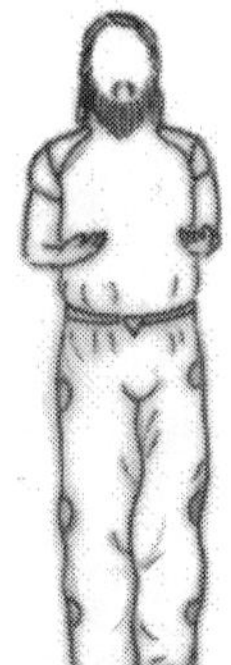

A-11

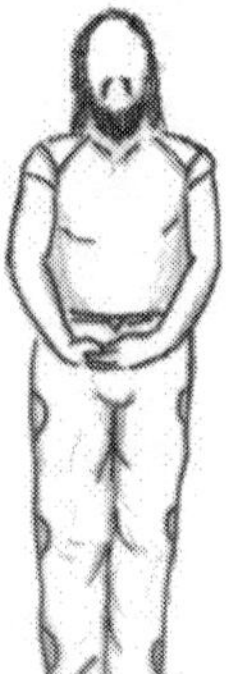

A-12

Resumen:
Seamm-Jasani: 8 Movimientos Fáciles

1. Turning Arms - Front
Relaxing the legs, inhaling
and exhaling normally
(count to 12)

2. Turning Arms – Lateral
Relaxing and bending the
legs, inhaling and exhaling
normally (count to 12)

3. Turning Arms – High
Relaxing and bending the
legs, inhaling and exhaling
normally (count to 12)

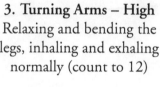

**4. Breathing Technique of
the Great Circle**
Inhale slowly, raising arms.
Contain. Exhale slowly,
lowering arms.
(2-3 times)

5 - Swimming Forward
Stretching forward, back straight,
as wide as possible
(12 Movements)

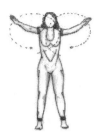

6 - The Machine
Begin slowly, then gradually
accelerate the speed of the
movement.
(20 seconds)

7 - To the Earth
Stretching Downwards
(3 times)

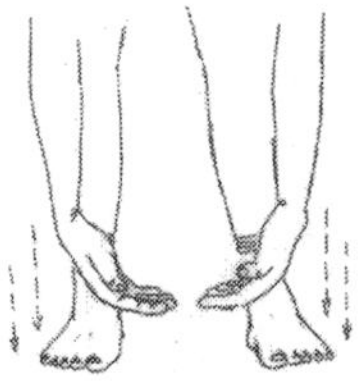

8 - To the Sky
Stretching Upwards
(3 times)

Seamm-Jasani Form: *Dawn*
Complete coordination from
Seamm-Jasani, beginning with
the feet together.
(3 times)

Jass-U©   Seamm-Jasani ©

28

Glossary

Boabom: ('bōä-'bom) Specifically Osseous Boabom, internal defense or energy, osseous force. The reference to 'osseous' indicates that the character or nature of this form of Boabom is like the bones: light, strong, and flexible.

Jass-U: Complementary system to Seamm-Jasani and Boabom that develops fluid exercises, relaxation, stretching, and breathing, helping to awaken the student's vitality.

Mmulargan: Literally translated as 'School,' the fundament of the Boabom teachings, or the circle at the root of the students and teachers of Boabom. Also a formal appellation for the Boabom Schools.

Seamm-Jasani: (se'am-m 'ha-'sa-ni) The perfection of quietude. Seamm-Jasani forms a part of the physical teachings of the Mmulargan Boabom. It is an Art of relaxation in movement, characterized by its use of slow and fluid coordinations in combination with various forms of breathing.

Yaanbao: The Art of the Elements. Focused on working with elements of various shapes and sizes, including but not limited to staffs of different lengths, swords, and other elements.

For more information about the Mmulargan Schools:

www.boabom.org

If you wish to contact a licensed teacher or to inquire about special intensive programs, please write to:

boabom@boabom.org

Seamm-Jasani ~ Boabom ©

Seamm-Jasani and Boabom Photo Album

OPEN CLASS, BOSTON, USA

BOSTON SCHOOL OF BOABOM   CLASSES AT MIT, USA

SEAMM-JASANI SEMINAR
IN NORWAY, EUROPE

NEW YORK, USA

OPEN CLASS, SANTIAGO, CHILE

QUITO, ECUADOR

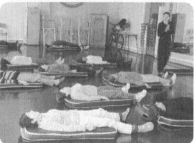

RELAXATION CLASS, CHILE

SEAMM-JASANI CLASS IN
LHASA, TIBET

TIBETAN STUDENT IN LHASA

31

About the Author

The author practicing Boabom in Yarlung, Tibet

Asanaro has dedicated more than twenty-five years to the study and transmission of the Boabom Arts, a path with roots in pre-Buddhist Tibet. The teachings in which Boabom is based upon are transmitted through various Arts, which cover breathing techniques, relaxation, defense, meditation, and philosophy.

He has taught around the world, offering courses, workshops, seminars and developing Schools in South America, Europe, Asia and the United States. He has also been instrumental in the founding and creation of various centers and associations that serve to stimulate interest in, and to advance the understanding of, these Arts.

Asanaro resides in the USA.

You can contact Asanaro via his website, or through email:

www.asanaro.com

asanaro@boabom.org

Other books by Asanaro

The secret art of
Seamm Jasani
Asanaro

The Secret Art of Seamm-Jasani
58 Movements for Eternal Youth from Ancient Tibet
A practical course-book in Seamm-Jasani.

(Tarcher/Penguin)

Boabom

The Secret Art of Boabom
An introduction to Boabom as philosophy and an Art of Defense

(Tarcher/Penguin)

BAMSO
THE ART OF DREAMS
ASANARO

Bamso, The Art of Dreams
Log of an Apprentice in the Art of Attaining Consciousness in Astral Voyages

(Tarcher/Penguin)

The Legend of the Mmulmmat

The Legend of the Mmulmmat
A book recounting the tale of a lost world in the ancient mountains of Tibet (The Valley of the Warm Breeze), describing the mythical origins of the Boabom teachings.

(AYA Publishing)

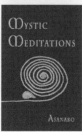

Mystic
Meditations
Asanaro

Mystic Meditations
A poetry collection of a different kind, consisting of powerful writings that invite the reader not only to enjoy their lyricism, but also to meditate and wonder.

(AYA Publishing)

Available only in Spanish

Manual de Cuidados Boabom

A guide for certified teachers of Seamm-Jasani and Boabom.
by Asanaro and the Boabom Council

(AYA Publishing)

Tibeñol

The first Spanish-Tibetan Dictionary
by Asanaro and Thupten Norbu

(AYA Publishing)

AYA Publishing - USA
http://www.ayapublishing.com/

An enormous positive energy for everyone!!!

May the cosmic winds always blow in your favor!!!

Boabom
An original drawing by Jamyang, Lhasa, Tíbet.
Dedicated to Boabom in commemoration of
the Tibetan New Year.

Made in the USA
Lexington, KY
17 October 2011